FIRST FRENCH

les animaux, mes amis

Consultant: Véronique Leroy-Bennett

LORENZ BOOKS

Contents

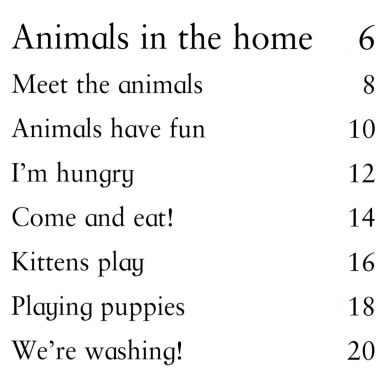

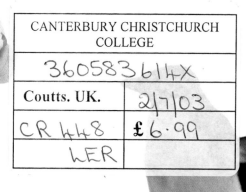

Learning French

Introduce your child to French from an early age by combining everyday words and phrases with lively photographs of animals big and small, on the farm, in the wild and around the home. Your child will enjoy learning French. Let them look at the pictures and read and remember the French words and phrases that accompany them. Say the words aloud.

 A NEW LANGUAGE

In our increasingly global society, the technology of communication evolves so fast that we are in contact with other countries more and more. There is a growing need to understand and speak a second language. For this reason, every child should have an opportunity early in life to have access to a new language. This book will support reading and writing during childhood and school years. Recent research indicates that children are most receptive to linguistic learning between the ages of two and eight. The younger the child, the easier it is to learn.

 PRACTISING TOGETHER

Children love animals, so this theme is a perfect one for introducing them to French. Encourage them to look at animals, birds and other creatures and say the French words aloud. They can use their new French vocabulary around the home with their pets, whenever they go out for a walk and at the zoo or nature reserve. You may have some French friends who can talk to your children. All this will give your children a brilliant head start when they begin formal French lessons at school.

LEARNING WITH PICTURES

Children respond very well to photographs and will enjoy finding pictures of their favourite animals in this book. Help them say and learn the French words for all sorts of pets, from cats and dogs to rabbits and guinea pigs. They'll discover the names of wild and farm animals, too, from giraffes, leopards and elephants to ducklings, sheep and pigs. Let them use French to count the animals or tell you what colours the animals are.

IT'S FUN TO LEARN

Make learning fun by using the vocabulary on an everyday basis. Children like to demonstrate what they have learnt by playing games. You could mime an animal or imitate the noise an animal makes and ask your child to say its name in French. Children can build up in a fun way their knowledge of commonly used French words and phrases. This will give them the confidence to speak French.

un

deux

trois

quatre

HOW THE BOOK IS STRUCTURED

The key words on each page are highlighted and translated in vocabulary panels. Sentences on each page appear in both French and English to help your child understand. At the end of every section is a question-and-answer game with a puzzle for you to do together and give the child a real sense of achievement. The dictionary lists all the key words and explains how they should be pronounced. Reward certificates at the end of the book encourage your child to test their knowledge of French and develop confidence and self-esteem.

Les animaux à la maison

Animals in the home are friendly.
Pets like to live with people.
Talk to playful puppies, naughty
little kittens and grown-up cats.
They'll understand you when
you speak French!

Rencontrer les animaux

Meet the animals and birds. They have heads and eyes and legs, just like us.

Bonjour. Je m'appelle Charlotte.
Hello. I am Charlotte.

Et moi, c'est Minette.
And I am Minette.

la fille

Charlotte

la queue

la tête

Minette

le chat

les yeux

la patte

	la fille	le garçon	la tête	les yeux
Say it with me	girl	boy	head	eyes

8

Que fais-tu, Félix?
What are you doing, Felix?

l'oiseau

Félix

Je vole comme un oiseau.
I am flying like a bird.

le garçon

le chien

Et moi, je saute.
And I am jumping.

la patte	la queue	le chat	le chien	l'oiseau
paw	tail	cat	dog	bird

Les animaux s'amusent

Animals have fun. They swim and jump just like us. But we can't fly – or make honey!

Regarde les abeilles!
Look at the bees!

l'antenne

cinq abeilles

l'aile

Elles font du miel.
They make honey.

le miel

Say it with me

l'antenne
antenna

l'aile
wing

cinq abeilles
five bees

le miel
honey

Je saute comme une grenouille.

I'm hopping like a frog.

quatre grenouilles

la jambe

la main

Nous pouvons nager comme des poissons.

We can swim like fish.

la nageoire

le poisson rouge

quatre grenouilles *four frogs*	la jambe *leg*	la main *hand*	le poisson rouge *goldfish*	la nageoire *fin*

J'ai faim

I'm hungry. The animals are hungry. Come and help the animals choose their favourite foods.

Simon

As-tu faim?
Are you hungry?

Oui, Simon, j'ai faim.
Yes, Simon, I am hungry.

le chien

la viande

Say it with me

le chien
dog

la viande
meat

les biscuits
biscuits

Que veux-tu manger?
What would you like to eat?

des biscuits?

des carottes?

le lapin

des oignons?

du fromage?

J'aime les carottes!
I like carrots!

les carottes	le fromage	les oignons	le lapin
carrots	cheese	onions	rabbit

A table!

Come and eat! Some animals like to be fed. Other animals catch their own dinner when they can.

Veux-tu une pomme?

Would you like an apple?

André

le lapin

la salade

Oui, s'il te plaît, André.

Yes, please, André.

le cobaye

Say it with me

la pomme	la salade	le lapin	le cobaye
apple	lettuce	rabbit	guinea pig

Qu'aimes-tu manger?
What do you like to eat?

du lait?

le chaton

deux souris?

trois poissons?

une glace?

Nous aimons les poissons.
We like fish.

le chaton	le lait	la glace	deux souris	trois poissons
kitten	milk	ice cream	two mice	three fish

Les chatons jouent

Kittens play. They like chasing wool, running after balls and jumping as high as they can.

Regarde le petit chaton!
Look at the little kitten!

J'aime jouer.
I like to play.

la chaise

le méchant chaton

Say it with me

la chaise
chair

le méchant chaton
naughty kitten

les jouets
toys

le chat roux
ginger kitten

les jouets

Attrape la souris!
Catch the mouse!

le chat roux   le chaton en peluche   le chaton qui saute

Nous jouons ensemble.
We are playing together.

le chat rapide

le chaton lent

la balle

chaton en peluche	le chaton qui saute	le chaton lent	la balle	le chat rapide
fluffy kitten	*jumping kitten*	*slow kitten*	*ball*	*fast kitten*

Les chiots jouent

Playing puppies never get tired! They love to run and play all day until it's time for bed.

J'amène mon chiot au parc.

I am taking my puppy to the park.

Est-ce que je peux venir aussi?

Can I come too?

la laisse verte

les pattes

l'os en caoutchouc

Say it with me

la laisse verte	l'os en caoutchouc	les pattes
green lead	rubber bone	paws

Nous jouons avec quatre balles.
We are playing with four balls.

un

deux

trois

le chiot

quatre

J'ai une grande balle bleue.
I have a big blue ball.

Je suis trop fatigué pour jouer.
I am too tired to play.

une grande balle bleue

le chiot endormi

trois balles bleues
three blue balls

le chiot
puppy

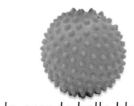

la grande balle bleue
big blue ball

le chiot endormi
sleepy puppy

19

Lavons-nous!

We're washing! Cats can spend hours washing themselves, and dogs like having their fur brushed.

Je me lave.
I am washing.

le shampooing

le bain

le savon

l'éponge

la serviette

les canards en caoutchouc

J'aime les bulles de savon.
I like soap bubbles.

Say it with me

le bain	le savon	la serviette	le shampooing
bath	soap	towel	shampoo

Nous sommes très propres!
We're very clean!

deux chiens

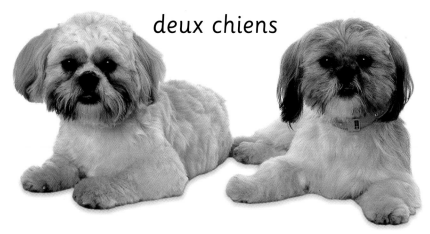

Je me brosse les cheveux.
I am brushing my hair.

la brosse à cheveux

Veux-tu me brosser le poil.
Will you brush me?

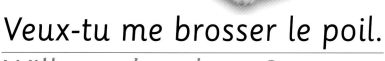

canard en caoutchouc rubber duck	l'éponge sponge	deux chiens two dogs	la brosse à cheveux hairbrush

C'est l'heure d'aller au lit

It's bedtime and everyone is tired. Let's get ready for bed and make sure the animals are comfy.

Bonsoir, tout le monde.
Good night, everyone.

le panier

le chat tigré

Nous sommes très fatigués.
We are very tired.

le chat rayé

Say it with me

le nounours
teddy bear

le panier
basket

le chat tigré
tabby cat

Je suis toujours fatiguée.
I'm always sleepy.

la tortue

Loulou

Bonbon et Belle

Qui dort dans le panier?
Who is sleeping in the basket?

le rêve

le chien brun

Je rêve.
I am dreaming.

le chat rayé	la tortue	le chien brun	le rêve
striped cat	tortoise	brown dog	dream

Puzzle time

Here are the animals you met, but can you remember their names? Here are some clues to help you. All their names are in the word square.

Le chiot marche.
The _ _ _ _ _ _ is walking.

Les poissons nagent.
The _ _ _ _ are swimming.

Le lapin mange.
The _ _ _ _ _ _ is eating.

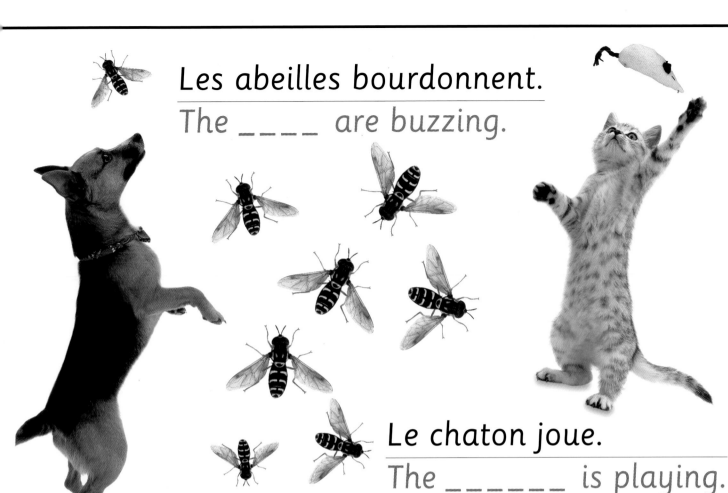

Les abeilles bourdonnent.

The _ _ _ _ are buzzing.

Le chaton joue.

The _ _ _ _ _ _ is playing.

Le chien saute.

The _ _ _ jumps.

Find all the French words in my word square

Où est le chat?

Where is the _ _ _ ?

a	s	c	a	t	g	p
b	c	h	a	t	l	o
e	h	i	e	r	a	i
i	i	e	i	n	p	s
l	o	n	l	o	i	s
l	t	p	l	a	n	o
e	c	h	a	t	o	n

Cherche les animaux

Look for the animals. You can find them in the home, in the garden and down on the farm. Look at the pictures and then say the words aloud. You're speaking French!

Où habitent t-ils?

Where do they live? Each animal has a favourite place to live. They feel safe inside their homes.

Le chiot vit dans un chenil.

The puppy lives in a kennel.

le chenil

Le chiot aime son chenil.

The puppy likes his kennel.

Say it with me

le chenil	la cage	le chat tacheté
kennel	cage	tortoiseshell cat

Quelle maison pour quel animal?
Which house for which animal?

le chat tacheté

la cage

les poissons rouges

l'aquarium

le hamster

le panier

les poissons rouges	le hamster	l'aquarium	le panier
goldfish	hamster	aquarium	basket

La maison de mes rêves

My dream home is beautiful! All these animals live in beautiful homes. Which one would you like?

Où habites-tu?
Where do you live?

la corde

le bateau

J'habite un bateau.
I live on a boat.

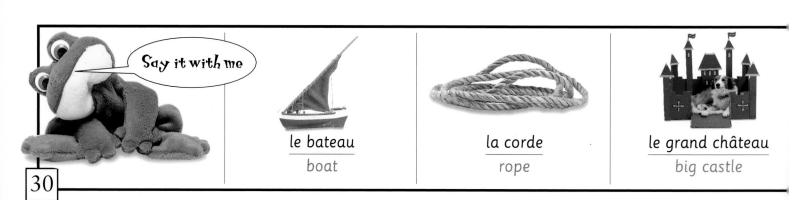

Say it with me

le bateau
boat

la corde
rope

le grand château
big castle

Nous vivons dans une petite maison.
We live in a little house.

le grand château

la petite maison

la porte

J'habite un grand château.
I live in a big castle.

l'appartement

la fenêtre

Nous habitons un appartement.
We live in a flat.

la petite maison
little house

l'appartement
flat

la porte
door

la fenêtre
window

Les bêtes du jardin

Garden creatures come in all sizes and colours!
Some get food from the plants in the garden.

Combien de papillons y a-t-il?

How many butterflies are there?

les papillons

la plante

le chat

le papillon bleu

Amélie

Il y a quatre papillons, Amélie!

There are four butterflies, Amélie!

Say it with me

la plante
plant

le papillon bleu
blue butterfly

le chat
cat

l'escargot
snail

Combien de bêtes dans chaque groupe?
How many creatures in each group?

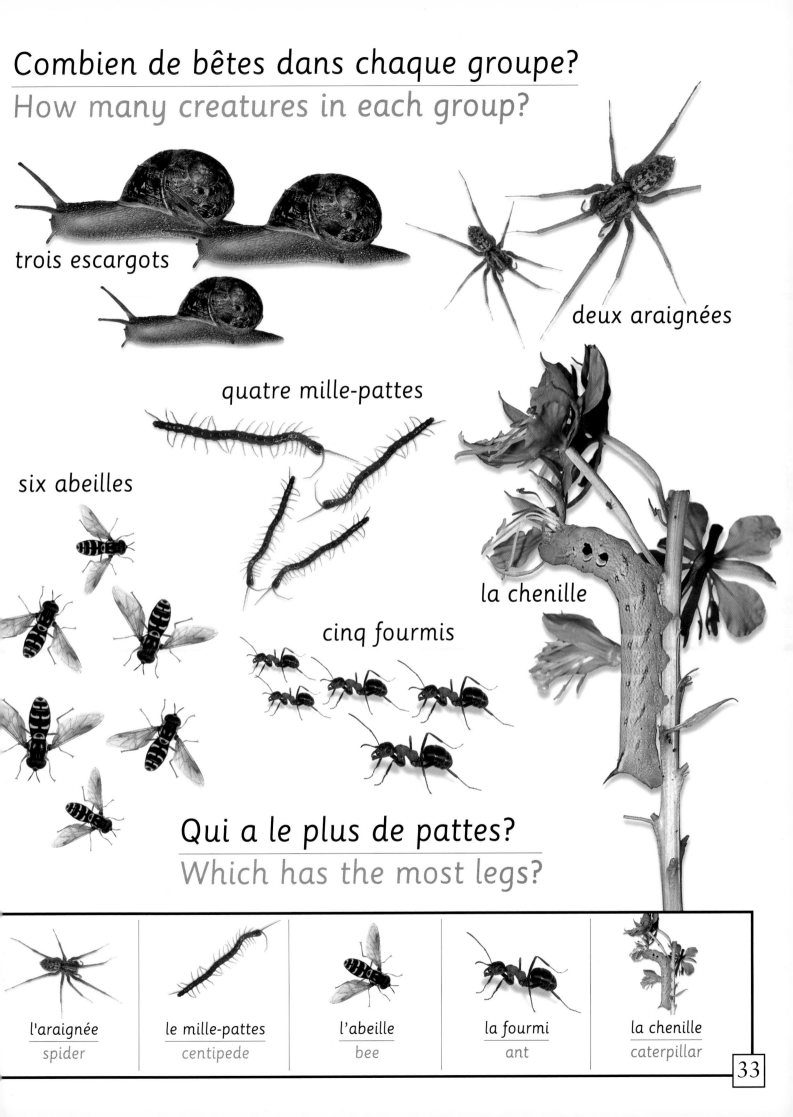

trois escargots

deux araignées

quatre mille-pattes

six abeilles

la chenille

cinq fourmis

Qui a le plus de pattes?
Which has the most legs?

l'araignée	le mille-pattes	l'abeille	la fourmi	la chenille
spider	centipede	bee	ant	caterpillar

Mes amis du jardin

Garden friends can be friendly or shy. You can put out food and water for the animals and birds.

Nous sommes dans le jardin.

We are in the garden.

les pots à fleurs

Plante de la salade, s'il te plaît!

Please plant some lettuce!

le lapin

le cobaye

Say it with me

le lapin
rabbit

le cobaye
guinea pig

les pots à fleurs
flowerpots

l'écureuil
squirrel

l'écureuil

Combien d'animaux y a-t-il?
How many animals are there?

les coccinelles

Il y a douze animaux.
There are twelve animals.

l'oiseau

la tortue

deux grenouilles

l'oiseau	l'arrosoir	la tortue	les coccinelles	la grenouille
bird	watering can	tortoise	ladybirds	frog

À la ferme

On the farm, it's fun to look after the animals.
There are lots of different animals and birds.

As-tu perdu ta maman?

Have you lost your mummy?

le veau

Oui, j'ai perdu ma maman.

Yes, I have lost my mummy.

Say it with me

le veau
calf

le cochon
pig

la vache
cow

Peux-tu aider ces mères à retrouver leurs bébés?
Can you help these mothers find their babies?

les canetons

la vache

le cochon

les poussins

le porcelet

la poule

le canard

le caneton	le poussin	le canard	le porcelet	la poule
duckling	chick	duck	piglet	hen

Les animaux à la ferme

Farm animals need to be cared for and fed. The sheepdog helps the farmer look after the sheep.

Que fais-tu?
What are you doing?

le chien de berger

le tracteur

Je cherche les moutons.
I am looking for the sheep.

Say it with me

le tracteur
tractor

le chien de berger
sheepdog

la ferme miniature
toy farm

Alice nourrit ses animaux.
Alice is feeding her animals.

Alice

la ferme miniature

Que mangent ces animaux?
What do these animals eat?

des pommes?

le mouton

de l'herbe?

le cheval

du foin?

la pomme	le mouton	l'herbe	le cheval	le foin
apple	sheep	grass	horse	hay

Puzzle time

Animals come in all shapes and sizes, but who is the biggest and who is the smallest? Complete the Lost Letters puzzle with their names.

Un hamster, est-il plus grand qu'une vache?

Is a _ _ _ _ _ _ _ _ bigger than a _ _ _ ?

Les fourmis sont très petites.

The _ _ _ _ are very small.

Christophe est-il plus petit qu'un caneton?

Is Christophe smaller than a _ _ _ _ _ _ _ _ ?

Un cheval, est-il plus grand qu'un chat?

Is a _ _ _ _ _ bigger than a _ _ _?

Find the lost French letters

Le lapin est petit.

The _ _ _ _ _ _ is small.

Le cochon est très gros.

The _ _ _ is very fat.

	c h e v a l
	v _ _ _ e
	c _ _ _ _ n
	_ _ a t
	c a _ e _ _ n
	_ _ p _ n
	f _ u _ _ _
	_ _ m _ t _ _

41

Parcourir
le monde

Around the world are many exciting animals. You can read about them now, and one day you may see them all. Get ready by learning their French names and saying the words aloud.

La forêt

The forest is a wonderful place to walk. You can find all sorts of wild animals.

Mathilde

Mathilde joue dans la forêt.
Mathilde is playing in the forest.

les noisettes

la pomme de pin

les feuilles

le lierre

Qu'est-ce qu'elle a trouvé?
What has she found?

Say it with me

les feuilles
leaves

la pomme de pin
pine cone

les noisettes
hazelnuts

les cloportes
woodlice

Combien d'animaux peux-tu voir?

How many animals can you see?

l'aigle

le hibou

le lapin timide

les cloportes

le renard

l'aigle
eagle

le hibou
owl

le lapin timide
timid rabbit

le lierre
ivy

le renard
fox

45

Au bord de la mer

On the seashore you can find all kinds of animals.
Look for them in rock pools and by the sea.

Nathalie

Qu'est-ce qu'elle cherche, Nathalie?
What is Nathalie looking for?

des coquillages

l'étoile de mer

le macareux

du sable

Say it with me

le coquillage
shell

le sable
sand

l'étoile de mer
starfish

le macareux
puffin

Qui nage dans l'eau?
Who is swimming in the water?

les mouettes

le soleil

les poissons

le dauphin

le crabe

la mouette
seagull

le soleil
sun

le poisson
fish

le crabe
crab

le dauphin
dolphin

La prairie

The grasslands are an exciting place to watch wild animals. But be careful not to get too close!

Patrice

les jumelles

Bonjour, Girafe. Comment ça va?
Hello, Giraffe. How are you?

la girafe

Ça va bien, Patrice, merci!
Very well, Patrice. Thank you!

Say it with me

les jumelles	la girafe	le zèbre
binoculars	giraffe	zebra

Qui a le nez le plus long?
Who has the longest nose?

le zèbre

le guépard

l'éléphant

le rhinocéros

la tarentule

le guépard
cheetah

le rhinocéros
rhinoceros

la tarentule
tarantula

l'éléphant
elephant

Dans la neige

In the snow, you'll find lots of animals that love the cold. Remember to wrap up warm!

le bonnet

l'écharpe

J'ai quelques boules de neige.
I have some snowballs.

Ne les jete pas sur nous!
Don't throw them at us!

les pingouins

les bottes

Say it with me

le bonnet
hat

l'écharpe
scarf

la boule de neige
snowball

la botte
boot

Attention!
Look out!

le phoque

les enfants

Nous nous cachons dans la neige!
We are hiding in the snow.

le hibou des neiges

l'ours blanc

le pingouin	le phoque	les enfants	le hibou des neiges	l'ours blanc
penguin	seal	children	snowy owl	polar bear

Les montagnes

The mountains can be wild and dangerous.
Look out for eagles and wolves.

Antoine

Regarde le faucon!
Look at the hawk!

l'imperméable

le faucon

Il ne m'attrapera pas, Antoine!
He won't catch me, Antoine!

le léopard

Say it with me

l'imperméable
raincoat

le faucon
hawk

le léopard
leopard

le vautour
vulture

Nous volons.
We are flying.

l'aile

le vautour

l'aigle

Je peux grimper.
I can climb.

les cornes

Je suis très féroce!
I am very fierce!

la chèvre

le loup

l'aile
wing

l'aigle
eagle

la chèvre
goat

la corne
horn

le loup
wolf

La jungle

The jungle is home to many brightly coloured animals. But you can't see them when they hide!

Je suis un tigre!
I am a tiger!

Quel beau perroquet!
What a beautiful parrot!

la plume

le perroquet

Say it with me

	la plume	le perroquet	la fourrure
	feather	parrot	fur

Qui est l'intrus?

Who is the odd one out?

le tigre

la fourrure

le serpent

C'est moi! Je n'ai pas de lignes!

It's me! I don't have stripes!

la grenouille

le caméléon

le tigre	le serpent	la grenouille	le camélèon
tiger	snake	frog	chameleon

Puzzle time

Patrice is trying to find animals of different colours. Can you help him fill in the sentences? Use the French words to fill in the crossword.

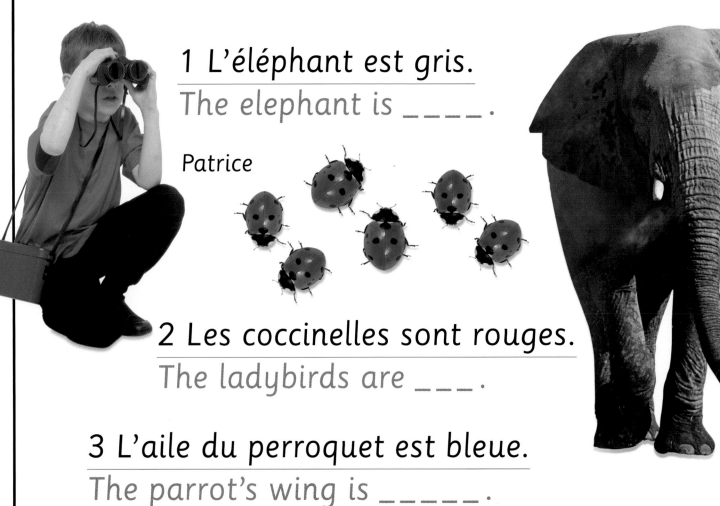

1 L'éléphant est gris.

The elephant is _ _ _ _ _.

Patrice

2 Les coccinelles sont rouges.

The ladybirds are _ _ _.

3 L'aile du perroquet est bleue.

The parrot's wing is _ _ _ _ _ _.

4 Le ventre du perroquet est jaune.

The parrot's chest is _ _ _ _ _ _ _.

5 La tarentule est brune.

The tarantula is _ _ _ _ _ _.

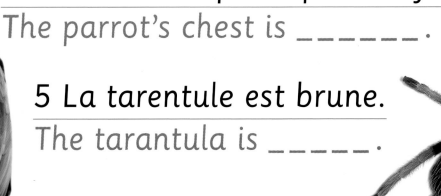

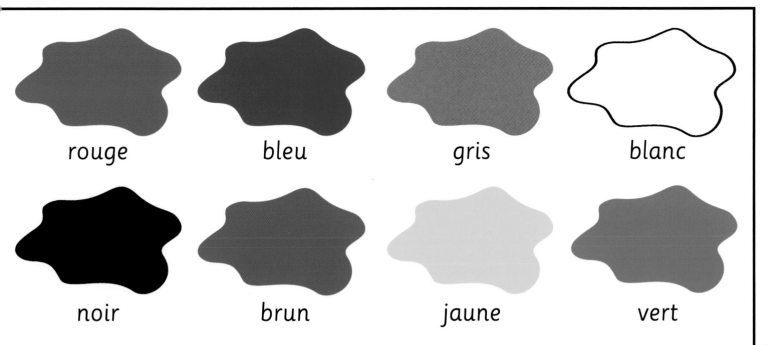

rouge   bleu   gris   blanc

noir   brun   jaune   vert

6 La tête du pingouin est noire.

The penguin's head is _ _ _ _ _ _ .

7 Le ventre du pingouin est blanc.

The penguin's chest is _ _ _ _ _ _ .

Now try my crossword!

8 La grenouille est verte.

The frog is _ _ _ _ _ _ .

How French works

Encourage your child to enjoy learning French and go further in the language. You may find these basic tips on how the French language works helpful. Check out the dictionary, since it lists all the key words in the book and will help you pronounce the words correctly to your child.

MASCULINE/FEMININE

All nouns in French are either masculine (le, un) or feminine (la, une), but this bears no relation to the actual gender of the animal (so a female tortoise is still le tortue). 'Les' or 'des' are for plural words whether they are feminine or masculine.

ADJECTIVES

As a general rule, an 'e' is added to the end of the adjective if the noun is feminine (e.g. 'la table verte'). Do not add an 'e' if the noun is masculine (e.g. 'le serpent vert').

COMPARING THINGS

When we want to compare things in English, we say they are, for example, small, smaller or smallest. This is the pattern in French:

FRENCH	ENGLISH
Il est petit	He is small
Il est plus petit que moi	He is smaller than me
Il est le plus petit	He is the smallest

petit

plus petite

la plus petite

PERSONAL PRONOUNS

Remember that 'il' is masculine and 'elle' is feminine. The plurals are 'ils' and 'elles'.

FRENCH	ENGLISH
je	I
tu	you (singular)
il *or* elle	he or she
nous	we
vous	you (plural)
ils *or* elles	they

'Tu' is used for talking to people you know or for talking to the animals and birds. 'Vous' is used when talking to someone you don't know and are being polite. It is also used when you are talking to more than one person.

Il est un garçon.

Elle est une fille.

 VERBS

French verbs change their endings depending on which personal pronoun and tense are used. This book uses only the present tense but there are other tenses in French including the past and the future.

Help your child find the language pattern that emerges in the endings of the verbs. Point out that in the verbs given here, 'tu' always ends '-es' and 'vous' always ends '-ez'. Explain that the extra 'e' in 'Nous mangeons' is to soften the 'g' and make it easier to say the words. Play a game by saying the first word aloud – 'Je', 'Tu'. Let your child answer with the verb – 'marche', 'marches'.

Here are four simple verbs in the present tense. Look at the ends of the words and say the French out loud.

FRENCH	ENGLISH
marcher	**to walk**
Je marche	I walk
Tu marches	You walk
Il/elle marche	He/she walks
Nous marchons	We walk
Vous marchez	You walk
Ils/elles marchent	They walk

FRENCH	ENGLISH
sauter	**to jump**
Je saute	I jump
Tu sautes	You jump
Il/elle saute	He/she jumps
Nous sautons	We jump
Vous sautez	You jump
Ils/elles sautent	They jump

FRENCH	ENGLISH
manger	**to eat**
Je mange	I eat
Tu manges	You eat
Il/elle mange	He/she eats
Nous mangeons	We eat
Vous mangez	You eat
Ils/elles mangent	They eat

FRENCH	ENGLISH
aimer	**to like**
J'aime	I like
Tu aimes	You like
Il/elle aime	He/she likes
Nous aimons	We like
Vous aimez	You like
Ils/elles aiment	They like

Pronunciation Key

FRENCH	PRONOUNCE	EXAMPLE
a, à	ah	pot à plante: po ah plon
an or en	on	blanc: blon
e, eu	uh	renard: ruh-nar
é	ay	réveil: ray-vehy
ê, è, ai	eh	tête: teht
eau, o, au	oh	dauphin: doh-fang
eil, eille	ehy	abeille: a-behy
euil, euille	euhy	feuilles: feuhy
g, ge, j	jsh	rouge: roojsh
gn	ny	oignons: o-nyon
i	ee	lit: lee
in	ah	lapin: la-pah
lle	y	chenille: shuh-neey
oi	wa	poisson: pwa-sson
on	on	chaton: sha-ton
ou	oo	loup: loo
ouille	ooy	grenouille: gruh-nooy
u	ew	tortue: tor-tew
ui	wee	cuillère: kwee-yehr
un	uhn	brun: bruhn

59

Le dictionnaire

ENGLISH	FRENCH	SAY

A

ant	la fourmi	*la foor-mee*
antenna	l'antenne	*lahn-ten*
apple	la pomme	*la pomm*
aquarium	l'aquarium	*la-kwa-reeum*

B

ball	la balle	*la bal*
balls	les balles	*leh bal*
basket	le panier	*luh pa-nee-ay*
bath	le bain	*luh bah*
bed	le lit	*luh lee*
bee	l'abeille	*la-behy*
bees	les abeilles	*leh za-behy*
big	grand	*grond*
binoculars	les jumelles	*leh jshew-mehl*
bird	l'oiseau	*lwaz-oh*
birds	les oiseaux	*leh zwaz-oh*
biscuits	les biscuits	*leh beess-kwee*
boat	le bateau	*luh ba-toh*
boot	la botte	*la bot*
boy	le garçon	*luh gar-sson*
boys	les garçons	*leh gar-sson*
butterfly	le papillon	*luh pa-pee-yon*

Colours

ENGLISH	FRENCH	SAY
black	noir	*nwar*
blue	bleu	*bluh*
brown	brun	*bruhn*
green	vert	*vehr*
grey	gris	*gree*
pink	rose	*rohz*
red	rouge	*roojsh*
white	blanc	*blon*
yellow	jaune	*jshonn*

Days of the week

ENGLISH	FRENCH	SAY
Monday	lundi	*luhn-dee*
Tuesday	mardi	*mar-dee*
Wednesday	mercredi	*mehr-kruh-dee*
Thursday	jeudi	*jshuh-dee*
Friday	vendredi	*vondruh-dee*
Saturday	samedi	*samuh-dee*
Sunday	dimanche	*dee-monsh*

ENGLISH	FRENCH	SAY

C

cage	la cage	*la kajsh*
calf	le veau	*luh voh*
carrots	les carottes	*leh ka-rot*
castle	le château	*luh sha-toh*
cat	le chat	*luh sha*
caterpillar	la chenille	*la shuh-neey*
centipede	le mille-pattes	*luh meel pat*
chair	la chaise	*la shehz*
chameleon	le caméléon	*luh kamay-lay-on*
cheese	le fromage	*luh fro-majsh*
cheetah	le guépard	*luh gay-par*
chick	le poussin	*luh poo-ssah*
children	les enfants	*leh zon-fon*
coat	le manteau	*luh man-toh*
cow	la vache	*la vash*
crab	le crabe	*luh krab*

D

dirty	sale	*sarl*
dog	le chien	*luh shee-ah*
dolphin	le dauphin	*luh doh-fah*
door	la porte	*la port*
dream	le rêve	*luh rehv*
duck	le canard	*luh ka-nar*
duckling	le caneton	*luh ka-nuh-ton*

ENGLISH	FRENCH	SAY
E		
eagle	l'aigle	*leh-gl*
ear	l'oreille	*lo-rey*
elephant	l'éléphant	*lay-lay-fon*
eyes	les yeux	*leh zyuh*
F		
fast	rapide	*ra-peed*
feather	la plume	*la plewm*
fin	la nageoire	*la najsh-war*
fish	le poisson	*luh pwa-sson*
fishes	les poissons	*leh pwa-sson*
flat	l'appartement	*la-par-tuh-mon*
flowerpot	le pot à fleurs	*luh poh a fluhr*
fluffy	pelucheux	*peh-lew-shuh*
fox	le renard	*luh ruh-nar*
frog	la grenouille	*la gruh-nooy*
frogs	les grenouilles	*leh gruh-nooy*
fur	la fourrure	*la foo-rewr*
G		
ginger	roux	*roo*
giraffe	la girafe	*la jshee-raf*
girl	la fille	*la feey*
girls	les filles	*leh feey*
goat	la chèvre	*la shehvr*
goldfish	les poissons rouges	*leh pwa-sson roojsh*
grass	l'herbe	*lehrb*
guinea pig	le cobaye	*luh ko-bay*
H		
hair brush	la brosse à cheveux	*la bross ah shuhvuh*
hamster	le hamster	*luh ham-stehr*
hand	la main	*la mah*
hat	le bonnet	*luh bo-neh*
hawk	le faucon	*luh foh-kon*
hay	le foin	*luh fwan*
hazelnuts	les noisettes	*leh nwa-zet*
head	la tête	*la teht*
hen	la poule	*la pool*
honey	le miel	*luh mee-ehl*
horn	la corne	*la korn*
horse	le cheval	*luh shuh-val*
house	la maison	*la meh-zon*

ENGLISH	FRENCH	SAY
I		
ice cream	la glace	*la glass*
ivy	le lierre	*luh lee-yer*
K		
kennel	le chenil	*luh shuh-neel*
kitten	le chaton	*luh sha-ton*
L		
ladybirds	les coccinelles	*leh kok-ssee-nehl*
lead	la laisse	*la lehss*
leaves	les feuilles	*leh feuhy*
leg	la jambe	*la jshomb*
leopard	le léopard	*luh lay-o-par*
lettuce	la salade	*la sa-lad*
little	petit	*puh-tee*
M		
meat	la viande	*la vee-ond*
mice	les souris	*leh soo-ree*
milk	le lait	*luh leh*
mouse	la souris	*la soo-ree*

Months of the year

ENGLISH	FRENCH	SAY
January	janvier	*jshon-vee-ay*
February	février	*fay-vree-ay*
March	mars	*marss*
April	avril	*av-reel*
May	mai	*meh*
June	juin	*jshew-ah*
July	juillet	*jshwee-eh*
August	août	*oot*
September	septembre	*sehp-tom-br*
October	octobre	*oc-tobr*
November	novembre	*no-vom-br*
December	décembre	*day-som-br*

ENGLISH	FRENCH	SAY
N and O		
naughty	méchant	*may-shon*
onions	les oignons	*leh zon-yon*
owl	le hibou	*luh ee-boo*

ENGLISH	FRENCH	SAY
P		
parrot	le perroquet	*luh peh-ro-keh*
paw	la patte	*la pat*
penguin	le pingouin	*luh pan-goo-ah*
pig	le cochon	*luh ko-shon*
piglet	le porcelet	*luh por-suh-leh*
pine cone	la pomme de pin	*la pomm duh pah*
plant	la plante	*la plahnt*
polar bear	l'ours blanc	*loorss blahn*
puffin	le macareux	*luh ma-ka-ruh*
puppy	le chiot	*luh shee-oh*

ENGLISH	FRENCH	SAY
R		
rabbit	le lapin	*luh la-pah*
raincoat	l'imperméable	*lahm-pehr-may-ahbl*
rhinoceros	le rhinocéros	*luh ree-no-say-ros*
rope	la corde	*la kord*
rubber bone	l'os en caoutchouc	*loss on ka-oo-tshoo*
rubber duck	le canard en caoutchouc	*luh ka-nar an ka-oo-tshoo*

Numbers

ENGLISH	FRENCH	SAY
1 one	un	*uhn*
2 two	deux	*duh*
3 three	trois	*trwa*
4 four	quatre	*katr*
5 five	cinq	*sahnk*
6 six	six	*seess*
7 seven	sept	*seht*
8 eight	huit	*weet*
9 nine	neuf	*nuhf*
10 ten	dix	*deess*

ENGLISH	FRENCH	SAY
S		
sand	le sable	*luh sa-bl*
scarf	l'écharpe	*lay-sharp*
seagull	la mouette	*la moo-et*
seal	le phoque	*luh fok*
shampoo	le shampooing	*luh sham-poo-ing*
sheep	le mouton	*luh moo-ton*
sheepdog	le chien de berger	*luh shee-ah duh behr-jshay*
shell	le coquillage	*luh ko-kee-yajsh*
sleepy	endormi	*ahn-dor-mee*
slow	lent	*lon*
small	petit	*puh-tee*
snail	l'escargot	*less-kar-goh*
snake	le serpent	*luh sehr-poh*
snowball	la boule de neige	*la bool duh nehjsh*
snowy owl	le hibou des neiges	*luh ee-boo deh nehjsh*
soap	le savon	*luh sa-von*
spider	l'araignée	*la-reh-nyay*
sponge	l'éponge	*lay-pon-jsh*
spotty	tacheté	*ta-shuh-tay*
squirrel	l'écureuil	*lay-kew-reuhy*
starfish	l'étoile de mer	*lay-twal duh mehr*
striped	rayé	*reh-yay*
sun	le soleil	*luh so-lehy*

ENGLISH	FRENCH	SAY
T and V		
tail	la queue	*la kuh*
tarantula	la tarantule	*la ta-ron-tewl*
teddy bear	le nounours	*luh noo-noorss*
tiger	le tigre	*luh tee-gr*
timid	timide	*tee-meed*
tortoise	la tortue	*la tor-tew*
towel	la serviette	*la sehr-vee-et*
toys	les jouets	*leh jshoo-eh*
tractor	le tracteur	*luh trak-tuhr*
vulture	le vautour	*luh voh-toor*

ENGLISH	FRENCH	SAY
W and Z		
watering can	l'arrosoir	*la-roh-zwar*
window	la fenêtre	*la fuh-nehtr*
wing	l'aile	*lehl*
wolf	le loup	*luh loo*
woodlice	les cloportes	*leh klo-port*
zebra	le zèbre	*luh zeh-br*

This is to certify that

_____

can count
from one to ten
in French

Date _____

This is to certify that

_____

can say
six colours
in French

Date _____

This is to certify that

_____

can say
six bird names
in French

Date _____

This is to certify that

_____

can say
six animal names
in French

Date _____

This edition is published by Lorenz Books

Lorenz Books is an imprint of Anness Publishing Ltd, Hermes House, 88–89 Blackfriars Road, London SE1 8HA
tel. 020 7401 2077; fax 020 7633 9499; www.lorenzbooks.com; info@anness.com
© Anness Publishing Ltd 2002

Published in the USA by Lorenz Books, Anness Publishing Inc.
27 West 20th Street, New York, NY 10011; fax 212 807 6813

This edition distributed in the UK by Aurum Press Ltd
25 Bedford Avenue, London WC1B 3AT; tel. 020 7637 3225; fax 020 7580 2469

This edition distributed in the USA by National Book Network
4720 Boston Way, Lanham, MD 20706; tel. 301 459 3366; fax 301 459 1705; www.nbnbooks.com

This edition distributed in Canada by General Publishing
895 Don Mills Road, 400–402 Park Centre, Toronto, Ontario M3C 1W3
tel. 416 445 3333; fax 416 445 5991; www.genpub.com

This edition distributed in Australia by Pan Macmillan Australia
Level 18, St Martins Tower, 31 Market St, Sydney, NSW 2000
tel. 1300 135 113; fax 1300 135 103; email customer.service@macmillan.com.au

This edition distributed in New Zealand by David Bateman Ltd
30 Tarndale Grove, Off Bush Road, Albany, Auckland
tel. (09) 415 7664; fax (09) 415 8892

Publisher: Joanna Lorenz
Managing Editor: Linda Fraser
Editors: Joy Wotton and Leon Gray
Design: Maggi Howells
Editorial Reader: Penelope Goodare
Photography: Jane Burton, John Daniels, John Freeman,
Robert Pickett, Kim Taylor, Lucy Tizard

The publishers would like to thank
all the children who appear in this book
and Martin B. Withers/FLPA – Images
of Nature for the photograph on
page 51 top right.

10 9 8 7 6 5 4 3 2 1